Rookie
Read-About®
Health

I Like to Exercise

by Lisa M. Herrington

Content Con

Catherine A. De

Reading Con

Jeanne M. Clid

Reading Spec

D1372425

Children's Press®
An Imprint of Scholastic Inc.
New York Toronto London Auckland Sydney
Mexico City New Delhi Hong Kong
Danbury, Connecticut

Library of Congress Cataloging-in-Publication Data
Herrington, Lisa M.
 I like to exercise/by Lisa M. Herrington.
  pages cm. — (rookie read-about health)
Audience: Ages 3-6
 ISBN 978-0-531-21011-6 (library binding: alk. paper) — ISBN 978-0-531-21068-0
(pbk.: alk. paper)
1. Exercise for children—Juvenile literature. I. Title.

 GV443.H45 2015
 613.7—dc23   2014035902

Produced by Spooky Cheetah Press
Design by Keith Plechaty

© 2015 by Scholastic Inc.

All rights reserved. Published in 2015 by Children's Press, an imprint of Scholastic Inc.

Printed in China 62

SCHOLASTIC, CHILDREN'S PRESS, ROOKIE READ-ABOUT®, and associated logos
are trademarks and/or registered trademarks of Scholastic Inc.

1 2 3 4 5 6 7 8 9 10 R 24 23 22 21 20 19 18 17 16 15

Photographs ©: iStockphoto: 31 center bottom (bjones27), 15 (CEFutcher), 8 (kirin_
photo), 24 (nycshooter), 28 bottom right (PhotoInc), 28 top right (termometrs), 28
bottom left (wsphotos); Media Bakery: 27, 29 (Fancy), 7 (Henn Photography), cover
(Ian Hooton); Shutterstock, Inc.: 3 bottom (Africa Studio), 28 top left (Len44ik),
3 top left (Lightspring); The Image Works/Daemmrich: 16; Thinkstock: 31 bottom
(Alexander Kosev), 30 (Anna Ziska), 20 (Fuse), 3 top right (Grata Victoria), 23
(Ingram Publishing), 4 (Jupiterimages), 19, 31 center top (monkeybusinessimages), 12,
31 top (Supertruper).

Illustration by Jeffrey Chandler/Art Gecko Studios!

Table of Contents

Get Moving!

I love to run, jump, and play.
Moving my body keeps me healthy.
I like to exercise!

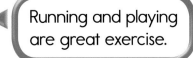

Running and playing
are great exercise.

When you exercise, your body is active. So turn off that TV, computer, or video game and get moving. Kids should get at least 60 minutes of exercise a day.

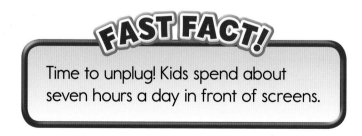

FAST FACT!

Time to unplug! Kids spend about seven hours a day in front of screens.

Why Exercise?

Exercise is an important part of being healthy. Being active makes you feel good about yourself. It helps you learn in school. It also helps you stay at a healthy weight.

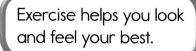

Exercise helps you look and feel your best.

Exercise makes your **muscles** strong. You have muscles all over your body. They pull on your **bones** to let you move. The more you move your muscles, the stronger they get. Even your heart is a muscle. It pumps blood around your body.

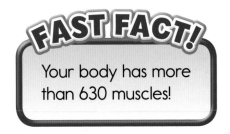

FAST FACT!

Your body has more than 630 muscles!

Your Body During Exercise

During exercise, your body uses up **oxygen**.

1. You breathe in oxygen from the air.

2. Your lungs breathe harder to take in more oxygen.

3. Your heart beats faster to carry oxygen in your blood to your muscles.

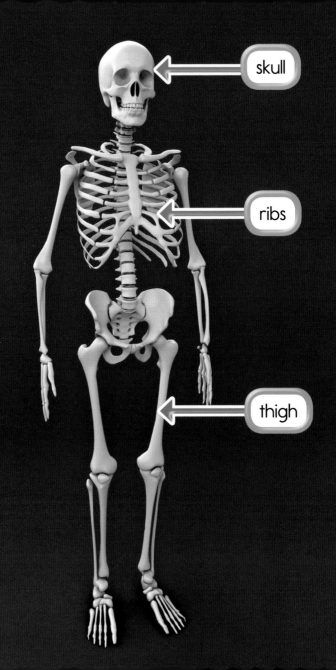

skull

ribs

thigh

Exercise builds strong bones.
Your bones hold you up.
Together, they are called the
skeleton. Your bones also protect
your insides. Your skull protects
your brain. Your ribs keep your
heart and lungs safe.

FAST FACT!

By adulthood, you will have 206 bones.
Your thigh bone is the longest.

Have Fun, Stay Fit!

Ready, set—move! There are lots of fun ways to stay in shape. Some kinds of exercise are good for your heart and lungs. Those activities include playing sports, swimming, and running.

Playing soccer can give your heart a good workout.

Playing sports is not the only way to get your heart pumping. Some kids like to ride a bike or skate. Others like to jump rope or dance. These are all good types of exercise.

You can even get exercise when you help out at home. So walk the dog. Rake leaves or sweep the sidewalk. Turn up the music and dance as you dust!

Pets need exercise, too. Walking the dog is good for you both!

Head outside to move your body.
Play hide-and-seek or hopscotch.
Toss a ball. Do yoga. Fly a kite.
Hike with your family. Go sledding
or ice-skating. What is your
favorite way to be active?
Just do what you enjoy most!

Having your whole family involved in the fun helps you stay fit together!

More Healthy Habits

Getting exercise is one part of taking care of yourself. You need **energy** to exercise. Eating good foods gives you energy. You should eat plenty of fruits and vegetables every day.

Your body needs a lot of water. It loses water through sweat when you are active. Make sure to drink water during exercise.

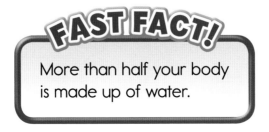

FAST FACT!

More than half your body is made up of water.

Regular exercise, healthy eating, drinking plenty of water, and getting enough sleep are all healthy habits that will make your body strong.

Exercise helps you sleep better, too!

Your Turn

Regular exercise keeps you healthy. Point to the picture in each pair that shows kids staying fit. What are they doing to be active?

1.

2.

Answers: 1. Taking the stairs instead of the escalator adds steps to your day. 2. Active play helps keep you healthy. Playing video games is not being active.

28

Feel the Beat!

While your body is at rest, place your hand over your heart. Can you feel your heart's steady beat? Now do 10 jumping jacks. Feel your heart again. What is the difference? Why, do you think, is your heart beating faster?

Answer: When you exercise, your heart works harder to pump oxygen-filled blood throughout your body.

Strange but True!

Did you know that sweating is good for you? Your body sweats when you exercise. Sweat is mostly water that comes through the skin. It works like an air conditioner. Its job is to cool you down.

Just for Fun

Q: What is harder to catch the faster you run?

A: Your breath!

Q: What does a frog like to do for exercise?

A: Jumping jacks!

Glossary

bones (bohns): hard, white body parts that make up the skeleton

energy (EN-ur-jee): the strength to be active without getting tired

muscles (MUHSS-uhls): body parts that help you move

oxygen (OCK-suh-juhn): a gas people breathe in from the air to live

Index

Facts for Now

Visit this Scholastic Web site for more information on exercise:
www.factsfornow.scholastic.com
Enter the keyword **Exercise**

About the Author

Lisa M. Herrington is the author of many books and articles for kids. Lisa lives in Trumbull, Connecticut, with her husband, Ryan, and daughter, Caroline. Her family enjoys being active outdoors.